For Jan with love from Gill

Can't Cook?

Then let's get you started!

Vegetarian and Vegan recipes for the complete beginner

Gill Emett Thomas

This book is dedicated to my spiritual guru Sri Chinmoy. He shared food with his disciples and cooked for them on many occasions. His teachings have brought joy and peace into my life.

Vegetarian or Vegan?

Vegetarians eat a plant based diet. They do not eat any kind of meat, fish or poultry as they do not want any living creature to be killed to provide their food.

Vegans want their diet to be entirely plant based and do not eat animal products such as dairy products, eggs or honey so vegan versions of some listed recipe ingredients are given.

Where milk is listed as an ingredient vegans can choose from a variety of plant based milks such as soya, almond or oat milk. Vegan cheese substitutes can also be used. Honey can be replaced by maple or agave syrup.

Anyone new to vegetarian or vegan diets can find invaluable information online. Google provides NHS guidelines for eating the necessary ingredients for good health.

Detailed information is provided to help you with any queries. For example, if you were interested in vegetarian or vegan sausages you could find a whole range of each of these products and be shown the stockists where you could buy them.

Many supermarkets and stores now stock a rapidly increasing number of vegetarian and vegan items.

Contents

Before You Begin 3
Success in the Kitchen 4
Stocking up in Stages 5
Stages 1-3 6
Store Cupboard Ingredients 7
Fresh Ingredients and Herbs 8
Cooking Utensils 9, 10
Washing up Kit, Serving up, Containers 11
Common Sense Hygiene 12
Getting to know your Cooker 13
Oven Temperatures, Weights and Measures 14

Soups 16
Chunky Vegetable 17
Tomato 19
Mushroom 21

Snacks 24
Non-cook meals 25
Bruschetta 26
Things on Toast 27
Sandwiches and Wraps 28

Breakfasts 30
Fruit Compote for Porridge 31
Make your own Granola 33
Make your own Muesli 33
Luxury Beans on Toast 35
The Big Breakfast 37

Main Meals 40
Stuffed Peppers 41
Tomato Tart 43
Lentil Chilli 45
Busy Week Baked Potatoes 47
Cottage Pie 49
Bulgar Wheat Pilaf 51
Noodle and Vegetable Stir-fry 53
Tomato Pasta 55
Baked Lemon Risotto 57
Quick Chickpea Curry 59
Barbecue Skewers 61
Roast Vegetables 63
Mung Bean Casserole 65

Salads 68
Spring Dandelion and Apple Salad 69
Fennel and Citrus Summer Salad 71
Rice, Shallot and Beetroot Winter Salad 73

Desserts 76
Super Simple Apple Crumble 77
Baked Nectarines 79
Fruit Jelly 81
Fruit Salads 83
Watermelon Treats 85
Celebration Trifle 87

Sources of Recipes 90
Index 91-93
Acknowledgements 94
Notes on Author 96

Before you Begin

If you haven't cooked before, check out that you will have: a level workspace, room in storage cupboards or on shelves for your ingredients and cooking utensils, and washing-up facilities. Will you have the use of a fridge and freezer for storing left-overs?

You may be living in a house, a flat or shared accommodation. Is there a cooker or separate oven and grill? Is there a microwave? Find out if there is some equipment already or if you could share some items. It is now possible to buy electric counter-top heaters which provide extra hobs for your kitchen.

Some of the cooking utensils you will need may be available already. Family or friends can sometimes let you have the odd spare item. Christmas or birthday presents could provide things like a hand-held blender or some cutlery. It's possible to find cooking utensils, attractive serving dishes or plates in charity shops. You may be fortunate in having a fully equipped kitchen, but if not, none of the recipes in this book require elaborate or expensive pieces of cooking equipment. A list of useful utensils is on page 9.

If you have something cooking in the oven do not wander off and forget it. Set a timer to go off to check the food half way through the cooking time, and then again for 10 minutes before the finish. Or set reminders on your phone.

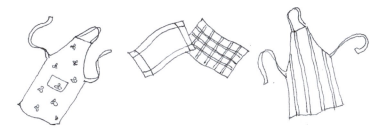

Success in the Kitchen

A few simple tips can make cooking fun and successful:

- Read your recipe the day before you begin. Check that you have all the necessary ingredients and utensils you will need, and dishes for serving up.
- On your working day assemble all the ingredients and utensils in one place before you begin.
- Always allow more time than you think you will need while you are still learning.
- Work neatly. Wipe spills as you go. Keep surfaces tidy. Return packages and jars to your storage area.
- Seasoning is always a matter of personal choice. It is better to under-season with salt, pepper, spices, chilli flakes etc, rather than to over-season which might spoil the dish. Adjustments can always be made later or at the table.
- Wash up as you go. For example, if your soup is on the stove and you need to keep an eye on it and stir it now and again, you can wash up while you are waiting for it to be ready. Clear vegetable peelings and wash up chopping knife and board and put away.
- After your meal deal with any remaining washing up. If you put your washed plates in a plate rack to drain that will cut down drying time. If cooking utensils have 'hard-to-clean' food deposits soak them in cold water for an hour and then use a pan scourer. Don't let your washing up get out of hand!
- Use an apron if you find them useful and keep a supply of clean drying cloths available.
- Leave your cooking area clean and tidy so that you really look forward to cooking there again.

Stocking Up in Stages

Suggested lists for:

- store cupboard ingredients
- fresh food supplies
- cooking utensils
- containers for left-overs
- plates and cutlery for serving

are on the following pages.

If you find these lists too daunting you could proceed by stages at a pace that suits you, as detailed opposite. This will be the easiest way forward if you are a complete newcomer to cooking.

Stage 1

Just try one recipe first - the **Chunky Vegetable Soup** on page 17. You will only need a few fresh vegetables, some frozen peas and little vegetarian stock pots. A large saucepan, knife and chopping board and some spoons are the only utensils you require, plus a storage container for any left-overs.

When you are confident with this soup you could try some of its variations on page 18.

While you are experimenting with these soups you can find plenty of suggestion in the **Snacks** pages (p25-28) which are helpful at this early stage.

In no time you will be able to produce soups as starters, or as a main meal, and could try simple **Non-Cook** salads (p71 and 72) and desserts (p83 and 86).

Stage 2

Lentil Chilli on page 45 is a good recipe to follow after the soup. You already have half the utensils required, although you will have to buy new ingredients.

You could also try the **Tomato Tart** on page 43, and the **Quick Curry** on page 59. So, by the end of Stage 2, you will have made soups, a lentil dish and a Tomato Tart and Quick Curry.

By backing up these recipes with the **Snacks** pages you will be able to make quite a range of meals of yourself, or to share with friends.

Stage 3

Continue to use the recipes tried in Stages 1 and 2 and add new recipes as you go. In this way you will gradually be stocking up your store cupboard, obtaining kitchen utensils, learning to use left-overs and taking on-board different cooking skills.

After this you can pick and mix any recipes that appeal to you as, by now, you have become more experienced and gained confidence in your own abilities.

Useful Store Cupboard Ingredients

- sea salt - coarse crystals and fine ground
- white and black pepper, paprika pepper, cayenne pepper
- carton of dried mixed herbs
- cartons of: ground cumin, ground coriander, chilli flakes, fennel seeds, curry powder, sesame seeds, ground turmeric
- ground spices - cinnamon, nutmeg
- vanilla extract, rum essence
- olive oil, rapeseed oil
- apple cider vinegar, balsamic vinegar
- tub of bouillon powder **or** stock cubes **or** little stock pots
- packet of red lentils
- tins of: kidney beans, baked beans, borlotti beans, chick peas, butter beans
- tins of green lentils
- tins of chopped tomatoes
- jar of roasted peppers in oil
- packet of rolled oats
- pumpkin seeds
- sunflower seeds
- sultanas, currants, raisins
- nuts of choice
- brown rice, arborio rice, long grain rice, wild rice
- pasta, including gluten free and wholemeal if liked
- sugars, including dark muscovado brown sugar
- honey or agave syrup, maple syrup
- sweet chilli sauce
- oat cakes, rice cakes or crackers
- packet of bulgur wheat
- packet quinoa
- packet couscous
- tins coconut milk
- tins coconut cream
- jar of coconut oil
- jars of pesto

Fresh Ingredients

- fresh fruit and vegetables - if you can buy these at local markets rather than supermarkets, they will often be fresher and cheaper
- milk of choice
- bread of choice
- butter or vegan alternatives
- onions and garlic
- fresh ginger root

Fresh Herbs

- parsley, mint, chives, basil - buy in packets to keep in the fridge or grow your own in a garden or on window sill
- buy other herbs as recipes require them

Cooking Utensils You Will Eventually Need

- three saucepans with lids - large, medium and a small non-stick one
- sieve
- grater
- large non-stick frying pan, medium frying pan
- two wooden spoons
- three sharp knives - one large, one small, one serrated
- measuring jug
- two large serving spoons
- measuring spoons - teaspoon, desert spoon, tablespoon
- two mixing bowls
- spatula
- chopping board
- whisk
- colander
- oven proof casserole dish with lid
- baking dish
- baking tray
- hand-held blender
- kitchen scissors
- fish slice
- can opener
- potato masher
- pastry brush
- wire cooling rack
- oven gloves or thick folded tea towel
- plastic lidded boxes for storage
- rolling pin
- microwaveable heat-proof bowl
- kitchen paper towels
- vegetable peeler

Kitchen Scales

Make sure your weighing scales have an easy to read dial or scale. You will need them for almost every recipe so keep them permanently on hand.

Washing Up Kit

- washing up liquid
- washing up brush
- washing up bowl
- sponges
- pan scourers
- tea towels
- rubber gloves - optional
- aprons - optional

For Serving Up

- cutlery
- plates
- bowls
- mugs
- cups and saucers
- glasses
- serving spoons and forks

Containers for Left-overs

- look for small, medium and large lidded containers that can store your left-overs in the fridge for a few days, or the freezer for weeks

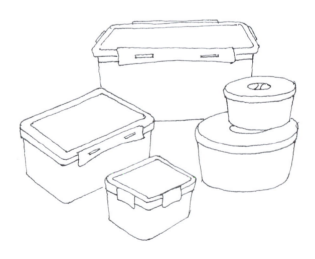

Common Sense Hygiene

- Before starting to cook wash your hands with hot water and soap. Repeat after cooking.
- Keep your cooking area clean. Wipe up spillages, crumbs and bits straight away from all work surfaces. Keep a separate cloth or mop for the floor.
- Do not overload your bin before emptying. Keep a good supply of bin liners. Keep your bin clean and disinfected inside and out.
- Wash cleaning cloths and tea towels regularly on a hot wash. Replace sponges and wiping down cloths regularly. If you drop a tea towel on the floor put it in the wash.
- Don't leave the washing-up to pile up and make a depressing clutter.

A clean, tidy, hygienic kitchen makes cooking safe.

Storing leftovers

If you are going to store surplus leftovers in your fridge or freezer, let them cool completely before putting in containers for storage. They will keep for two to three days in your fridge, or three months in your freezer

Defrosting leftovers

Make sure any left-over food that was stored in your freezer is defrosted before you re-heat it. Place the frozen food in its container on a plate in the fridge overnight and then finally defrost it at room temperature in the kitchen.

Re-heating leftovers

When re-heating leftovers make sure they are piping hot before serving (not just warm!).

Only reheat food once - any leftovers must not be put back in fridge or freezer again.

Understanding Your Cooker

Whichever kind of cooker you will be using, you need to get to know its particular characteristics. You will find that some cookers do vary a little in performance, so be watchful, use common sense and make adjustments if necessary.

For instance, until you get to know your oven, if your chosen recipe says that something needs baking in the oven for 40 minutes, check 10 minutes before. Occasionally you may have to cook 10 minutes or so longer.

Look at the chart opposite to see the temperatures for electric ovens, fan ovens and gas ovens to match with YOUR cooker, and the instructions in your chosen recipe.

Whichever kind of cooker you are using you will soon learn how to adjust the temperature of the hobs using the chart below as a guide.

Using **soup** as an example look at the chart below:

Low	The surface of the soup will be **very** gently agitated and there may be slight steam.
Medium	There will be steady heat, some slight bubbling and agitation of the soup's surface and more steam. The soup will cook at a 'simmer'.
High	Food will boil. There will be strong agitation, fierce bubbling and steam. The soup may rise up the sides of the pan to overflow. Also it may burn if not stirred and watched. **Do not wander off if food is boiling.** If necessary remove from heat or reduce temperature.

Oven Temperatures

Electric		Fan Oven		Gas Mark
°C (centigrade)	°F (Fahrenheit)	°C (centigrade)	°F (Fahrenheit)	
110	230	90	194	¼
130	266	110	230	½
140	284	120	248	1
150	302	130	266	2
170	338	150	302	3
180	356	160	320	4
190	374	170	338	5
200	392	180	356	6
220	428	200	392	7
230	446	210	410	8
240	464	220	428	9

Liquids

Metric	Imperial
5ml	1tsp
15ml	1tbsp
25ml	1fl oz
50ml	2fl oz
100ml	3½fl oz
125ml	4fl oz
150ml	5floz/¼ pint
175ml	6fl oz
200ml	7fl oz
250ml	9fl oz
300ml	10floz/½ pt
450ml	15lfoz/¾ pt
600ml	1 pint
900ml	1½ pints
1 litre	1¾ pints

ml = millilitres

Measures

Metric	Imperial
5mm	¼in
1cm	½in
2cm	¾in
2.5cm	1in
3cm	1¼in
4cm	1½in
5cm	2in
7.5cm	3in
10cm	4in
15cm	6in
18cm	7in
20.5cm	8in
23cm	9in
25.5cm	10in
28cm	11in
30.5cm	12in

cm = centimetres

Weights

Metric	Imperial
15g	½oz
25g	1oz
40g	1½oz
50g	2oz
75g	3oz
100g	3½oz
125g	4oz
150g	5oz
175g	6oz
200g	7oz
225g	8oz
250g	9oz
275g	10oz
300g	11oz
350g	12oz
375g	13oz
400g	14oz
425g	15oz
450g	1lb
550g	1¼lb
700g	1½lb
900g	2lb
1.1kg	2½lb

g = grams

Don't forget …

Ovens and grills **MUST** be pre-heated to the specified temperature **BEFORE** you put the food in.

Soups

These soup recipes make enough for three to five people depending on their appetite ... for example, teenagers and young students will probably want much larger portions than many elderly people.

If you don't want all the soup on the day that you make it, you will find it very useful to have surplus soup stored in the fridge or freezer to provide a quick meal in a hurry another day.

Soups

Chunky Vegetable.. 17

Tomato 19

Mushroom... 21

Chunky Vegetable Soup for four

Ingredients

Two medium carrots • Two medium parsnips • Two medium leeks • Two sticks celery • Packet frozen peas • Parsley • Butter or vegan spread • Veg Stock pots

Utensils large saucepan • chopping knife • chopping board • one mug • one dessert spoon • one wooden spoon • kitchen scissors • measuring jug

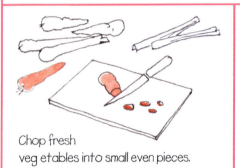

Chop fresh vegetables into small even pieces.

Melt 25g of butter or vegan spread in a large saucepan on a low to medium heat. Add chopped vegetables and fry for 5-6 minutes, using the wooden spoon to stir them. Turn them over constantly to avoid browning. Remove from the heat.

Pour boiling water onto the contents of 1½ vegetable stock pots to make 800mls of stock. Pour over the chopped vegetables. Store remaining half stock pot in fridge.

Bring your soup to the boil. Now turn down the heat to medium and add one mug of frozen peas and stir through. Put the lid on the pan and cook gently for 15 minutes.

Snip sprigs of parsley with kitchen scissors to stir through your soup.

Spoon soup into bowls. Store any surplus soup (cooled completely) in lidded containers in fridge or freezer.

Useful Variations

- For a main meal eat this soup with crusty bread, butter and cheese, or with a non-dairy spread and vegan cheese. Alternatively you could eat toast spread with hummus. Follow with a piece of fruit.

- Add a large dollop of creamy mashed potato on top of the soup and sprinkle with chopped parsley.

- You can 'green-up' your soup by choosing from any of the following: chopped green beans, small florets of cauliflower or broccoli, finely chopped kale. Cook these green vegetables in a small saucepan of boiling salted water until tender (6-10 minutes), drain and add to soup.

- Thin your soup with extra hot vegetable stock (made with bouillon powder, stock cube or stock pot) in which you have cooked pasta shapes to add to the mix.

- Alter the texture of this chunky soup by using a hand-held blender to produce a smooth version. Top with a swirl of cream, crème fraiche or plain soya yoghurt and chopped parsley.

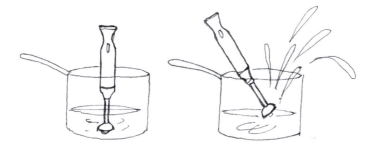

Make sure to hold your blender upright with the rotating blades under the surface of the soup.

Blend in short bursts. Don't rest blender on bottom of saucepan. It takes a bit of practice. Some people like to blitz half the soup in a jug and then add it to the remaining chunky soup.

Tomato Soup for four

Ingredients

Two red onions

Six tomatoes

Tin of coconut milk

One garlic clove

Tomato puree

Olive oil

Sea salt and pepper

Utensils chopping board • chopping knife • large saucepan • roasting tray • handheld stick blender

Pre-heat oven 200°C or 392°F electric, 180°C or 356°F fan, gas mark 6.	Chop the onions and tomatoes roughly. 	Cut the top off the garlic bulb. Place on a square of foil. Spoon olive oil generously over garlic bulb. Then wrap foil over completely to make a neat garlic parcel. 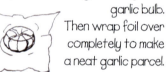
Place the onions, tomatoes and garlic parcel in a lightly oiled roasting tray.	Roast for one hour. The onions may only need 45 minutes. Check now and again and remove from tray when done.	Squeeze the roasted garlic flesh from the bulb and add to the large saucepan, together with the onions, tomatoes, half a tin of coconut milk, half a tin of water and one tablespoon of tomato puree.
Mix the contents of the pan together. Season with salt and pepper to taste. Cook gently for 10 minutes.	Blend the contents of the pan with the stick blender. Remember to keep the blender upright. See WARNING on page 18.	 This soup freezes well. Or store in fridge for more immediate use.

Another Batch Soup

This makes enough for six people.

A comforting soup to make for a cold winter's day, with surplus to store.

Leek and Potato Soup

1 medium onion
3 cloves of garlic
2 large leeks
4 unpeeled potatoes
2 tablespoons oil
2 teaspoons of sea salt
1 bay leaf
2 litres of vegetable stock
½ teaspoon black pepper
Juice of ½ lemon

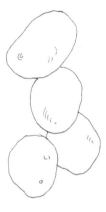

Prepare   Finely slice onion and garlic.
Chop potatoes and slice the leeks, including part of the green leek tops. You will need to clean inside the leeks carefully to remove any soil.

Cook   Heat the oil in a large saucepan, add the garlic and onion and cook for three minutes stirring all the time. Add the potatoes and leeks, salt and bay leaf to the pan and cook together for five minutes.
Add the stock and black pepper - bring to the boil, then reduce the heat to a simmer for a further 15 minutes, or until the potatoes are soft.

Blend   Remove from the heat, take out the bay leaf and blend with stick blender.
Check seasoning and add a squeeze of lemon to each bowl when serving.

Mushroom Soup for four

Ingredients

Parsley

Butter or vegan spread

One onion
One green pepper
One leek

Vegetable stock cube

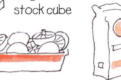
Mushrooms
Two cloves garlic

Plain flour

Milk of choice

Utensils knife • chopping board • tablespoon
large saucepan • wooden spoon • measuring jug

Chop the onion, green pepper, leek and garlic finely.	Melt 25g butter or vegan spread  in a large saucepan.	Add the chopped vegetables and garlic and cook gently, stirring now and again until they start to soften.
Slice 300g mushrooms  into thin slices.	Increase the heat in the pan, then add the mushroom slices and cook, stirring until they are cooked through.	Stir in two tablespoons of plain flour for one minute until all the flour is absorbed into the mix.
Make 450ml of hot vegetable stock using a stock cube and hot water Add gradually to pan, stirring as you go.	Bring the pan of vegetables and stock to the boil, then reduce heat and cook gently for three minutes. Pour in 450ml milk and simmer for a few minutes.	 Add plenty of chopped parsley. Season to taste.

Eating Mushrooms

There are very many different kinds of mushrooms. For the recipe opposite you could use small white button mushrooms or chestnut mushrooms which tend to have more flavour. Both would be suitable for this recipe.

White button mushrooms **Brown chestnut mushrooms**

Mushrooms do not need washing before use. Just remove any fragments of soil with a paper towel.

Large flat field mushrooms are fried for the Big Breakfast recipe on page 37.

These field mushrooms are also very good baked. Pre-heat the oven to 190° electric, fan 170° or gas Mark 5.

Place the mushrooms, gill side up, in a small oiled dish. Dot each mushroom with butter, scatter a little finely chopped garlic on them, then lightly season with sea salt and pepper. Bake for 15-20 minutes until juicy.

These make a very good snack, with or without grated cheese on top before cooking, or are useful to accompany other dishes.

Never use mushrooms that you have picked in the wild yourself unless you are **quite certain** you can identify those which are not poisonous.

Snacks

This is a particularly helpful section for beginners as it is more about putting things together than learning cooking processes.

You can be quite innovative in what you put together to suit yourself.

Snacks

Non-cook meals 25

Bruchetta 26

Things on Toast 27

Sandwiches and Wraps 28

Non-Cook Meals

If sometimes you haven't the time to cook, it is possible to put together a delicious healthy meal without cooking at all.

For example - assemble different breads, oatcakes, rice cakes or crackers with butter or a spread of your choice. Choose from one or two of your favourite cheeses, chutneys and pickles, or a bowl of olives. Sticks of trimmed celery and ripe tomatoes can complete the selection.

Follow with fruits of your choice: raspberries, strawberries, grapes, blueberries, ripe nectarines or plums, a slice of melon or pineapple, crisp eating apples or a banana. Eat as they are or sliced with a helping of coconut vegan yoghurt, or a choice of dairy yoghurts.

This kind of impromptu meal can sometimes be a treat, needing very little preparation or clearing up.

Bruschetta

Requiring very little cooking time bruschetta can make a satisfying quick lunch or supper.

You will need thick slices of sourdough bread or ciabatta. Toast very lightly on both sides and rub the top of each piece with a cut clove of garlic. Drizzle the top of each piece of toast with olive oil. Keep warm.

There are countless toppings to choose from. To start you could choose from:

- **Red peppers and soft cheese**

    Spread the toasted bread with sundried tomato pesto. Top with pieces of red pepper from a jar (very well drained and patted dry with kitchen paper) and small slices of soft cheese. Season to taste.

- **Tomato and Avocado**

    Spread the toasted bread with basil pesto from a jar. Top with slices of tomato and avocado (brush the avocado slices with lemon juice to stop them turning brown). Finish with small chunks of mozzarella or feta cheese, or vegan equivalent, if you like.

- **Courgette and Thyme**

    Cook slices of two courgettes in a small frying pan in a couple of spoonfuls of olive oil with a pinch of salt until they are soft. Mash the courgettes a little and add a sprinkling of black pepper and a squeeze of lemon juice. Pile on toast with a trickle more of olive oil and scatter with thyme leaves.

Things on Toast

Practice making golden toast using a toaster or the cooker's grill pan, trying a variety of breads. Select butter or a vegan spread to put on the toast before adding your topping.

Three savoury toppings to try

- The two flat field mushrooms shown with their cooking instructions on page 22) would make a good snack.

- Take 120 grams of really ripe sweet tomatoes of any size and cut them into small even sized chunks. Place in a bowl with a dessertspoon of olive oil, a pinch of sugar and just a **little** black pepper. Toss together, then pile on your toast. Scatter with chopped herbs (either mint, parsley or chives) and a few flakes of crunchy sea salt.

- Baked beans, heated in a saucepan straight from the tin, have always been a useful standby.

  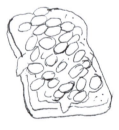

Sandwiches

Another quick non-cook solution to a meal in a hurry is to make sandwiches.

Select a favourite bread and spread and choose a filling: nut butter and banana, hummus and sliced olives, sliced cheese and tomato, blue cheese and watercress, mashed avocado and tomato, grated cheese and chutney ... and so on. You could invent your own fillings.

Make a couple of your favourite and follow with a piece of fresh fruit.

Tortilla Wraps

A tortilla is a type of thin unleavened flatbread made from corn or wheat and, because it is soft and flexible, it lends itself to rolling and folding.

You have a wide choice of fillings: tomato, different cheeses (sliced thinly, chopped or grated), beans, cooked onions, avocado, peppers, sweetcorn, salad ingredients, sliced vegetarian or vegan ham or sausage and many more.

There are two ways of making your wraps.

In the first the tortilla is folded over a central chunky filling and is best eaten with a plate to hand.

In the second version spread a **thin** layer of creamy dressing, tomato puree, hummus, soft cheese or pesto over the tortilla base. Then sprinkle your filling ingredients all over, fold in the sides and roll up from the bottom before cutting into sections.

Breakfasts

These breakfasts range from one with no cooking required at all, to more elaborate recipes for those days when you have time for a more leisurely breakfast.

Breakfasts

Fruit Compote for Porridge 31

Make your own Granola 33

Make your own Muesli 33

Luxury Beans on Toast 35

The Big Breakfast 37

Fruit Compote for Porridge

Ingredients

One cooking apple

Water

Apple juice

One Lemon

Cinnamon and nutmeg

Two cloves

Dried fruit

Dried apples, pears, prunes, apricots and sultanas

Rolled porridge oats

Milk of choice

Utensils

measuring jug • teaspoon • knife • grater
two saucepans • wooden spoon • scales

Peel and core the apple and cut into pieces.

Grate lemon rind from ¼ of the lemon.

Warm 70ml apple juice and 30ml water together - add ¼ teaspoon cinnamon, two cloves and a pinch of grated nutmeg.

Add 50g of dried fruit, the lemon rind and apple.
Cook on gentle heat for 20 minutes until all the fruit is soft.
Remove cloves and leave to cool.

Mix together:
80g rolled oats
225ml milk of choice
225ml water
Bring gently to boil stirring frequently.
Simmer five minutes still stirring to make porridge.

Top porridge with some fruit compote, storing any surplus compote in the fridge or freezer. Can be sweetened with a little honey if liked.

Fresh berries such as blueberries, raspberries or strawberries could make an alternative porridge topping.

Wholegrain Porridge Oats

Ideas vary widely about ways to make and serve porridge. To start with you could make it using the method on the opposite page marked with a ⭐ .

Some people use all milk, others half milk to half water, others water alone but served with milk.

Some like to serve it with: a sprinkling of salt and no sugar; a dusting of brown sugar; a topping of berries or fruit compote; sliced banana; with a few snipped ready-to-eat prunes or apricots stirred through while cooking ... and so on.

If you want to make your porridge in the microwave follow instructions on the oats package.

However you make and serve it, porridge is a nourishing food which keeps you feeling satisfied for quite some time afterwards.

Wholegrain oats provide soluble fibre for healthy digestion and release their energy very slowly which is why you feel fuller for longer.

Perhaps even more importantly the beta-glucan in wholegrain oats has been shown to lower cholesterol to support a healthy heart.

An all round winner!

Make your own Granola

Ingredients

 Sunflower seeds

 Pumpkin seeds

 Chopped nuts of choice

Sunflower oil

 Soft ready to eat dried apricots

 Sultanas or raisins

Runny honey or maple syrup

 Rolled oats

Utensils large spoon • small saucepan • baking tray • whisk • baking parchment • large bowl

Pre-heat oven 150°C or 302°F electric, 130°C or 266°F fan, gas mark 2.	Heat 150g honey or syrup with eight tablespoons sunflower oil in the small saucepan. Bring to the boil whisking together.	Into the bowl put 225g rolled oats, 100g mixed seeds, 100g chopped nuts. Pour the hot liquid over the dry ingredients and mix thoroughly.	Cover the baking tray with baking parchment and spread the granola mixture over evenly. Cook 45 minutes in pre-heated oven, turning now and again to brown.
When cold break up into small pieces. Add 25g sultanas and 25g of finely chopped dried apricots to the mix		Add spoonfuls of granola to servings of fruit and yoghurt or milk of choice.	Store surplus granola in an airtight jar in a cool dry place.

Make your own Muesli

Mix the ingredients of the jar together to make your museli. Eat spoonfuls with milk of your choice and sliced banana or berries.

Fill a large screw top jar three-quarters full of rolled oats. Fill the remaining one quarter with your choice of seeds, nuts and dried fruit.

Breakfast Fruits

Caramelised Apple Slices

These delicious apple slices can be used to top your porridge or muesli.

Place two peeled, sliced and cored Granny Smith apples in a frying pan with a teaspoon of ground cinnamon and three tablespoons of maple syrup. Bring to a gentle simmer and cook until the apple slices are soft and sticky. Watch them carefully to prevent them burning and turn constantly to cook all sides. Serve warm or cold.

Poached Plums

Pour 200ml of cold water into a saucepan. Add 100g of caster sugar and gently bring to the boil, stirring to dissolve the sugar. Simmer for a few minutes. Add 600g of washed and halved (or sliced) plums and poach gently until they are soft, then let them cool in their own syrup. These are delicious served cold with thick yoghurt of your choice, or on cereals. Store any surplus fruit in the fridge or freezer.

Luxury Beans on Toast for four

Ingredients

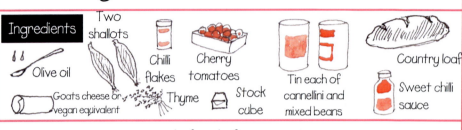

Two shallots, Olive oil, Goats cheese or vegan equivalent, Chilli flakes, Cherry tomatoes, Thyme, Stock cube, Tin each of cannellini and mixed beans, Country loaf, Sweet chilli sauce

Utensils large saucepan • knife • knife • measuring jug • tin opener • toaster or grill pan of cooker

Peel skin from shallots and cut them into quarters. See page 73.

Chop shallots finely

Heat two tablespoons oil in a large pan and fry the chopped shallots and half teaspoon of chilli flakes for two minutes, stirring gently.

Halve 150g of cherry tomatoes. Make 125ml of hot vegetable stock with hot water and half the stock cube. Stir to dissolve.

Add the drained beans, tomatoes, two tablespoons of sweet chilli sauce, the stock and some of the thyme leaves to the saucepan. Season and heat until the tomatoes soften.

Meanwhile toast eight slices of bread of choice.

Put two slices of toast onto each of the plates and spoon over the bean mix, together with any pan juices. Crumble 50g of cheese to share between the four plates as a topping and a few thyme leaves.

Breakfast Toast

Try making toast using different kinds of bread:

- Thin white sliced
- White country loaf
- Sourdough bread
- Wholemeal
- Seeded bread
- Gluten free bread ... and so on

to discover your favourites. Different breads suit different toppings.

You can spread your toast with butter or vegan spreads, pestos, nut butters, or mashed avocado for savoury toppings.

Breakfast toast is also very good with butter or vegan spread topped with jams, preserves, honey or syrup.

* There are some simple meals in the Snacks section which would make quick easy breakfasts – mushrooms on toast page 27, tomatoes on toast page 27, or some of the Bruschetta on page 26.

The Big Breakfast for one

Ingredients

Two large tomatoes

Vegan or vegetarian sausages

Rapeseed oil

Two flat mushrooms

Small tin of baked beans

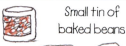
Two slices of sourdough bread

Utensils
large frying pan • small saucepan • wooden spoon fish slice • two serving plates

Turn the oven or grill on VERY LOW to warm the two plates. As you cook your ingredients put them on the top warmed plate until needed.	First cook the sausages in a frying pan on a medium heat in a spoonful of rapeseed oil, turning now and again until done, approximately six to eight minutes.	Remove the sausages to the warmed plate when done and add the halved tomatoes and the mushrooms to the pan. Add a little more oil if necessary. Cook until tender.
Remove cooked tomatoes and mushrooms to the warmed plate. At this stage you could turn the oven or grill off, keeping the oven door closed to retain warmth.	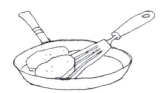	Increase the heat under the frying pan a little and fry the bread slices until crispy before adding to the other warmed ingredients.
Heat the baked beans in the small saucepan. Assemble the cooked sausages, tomatoes, mushrooms and fried bread neatly on the second clean plate and add the baked beans.	 Serve with juice, toast and marmalade for a big brunch, and your choice of tea or coffee if liked.	

The Big Breakfast

You can still make yourself a 'traditional' big breakfast now and again.

Sometimes you can combine breakfast and lunch into one meal or 'brunch', this is enjoyable on your own or sharing with friends.

If you are sharing with friends, increase all the ingredients of choice in proportion to the number coming.

Search out some good vegan or vegetarian sausages. Choose sourdough bread or good thick slices of other vegan bread for your fried bread.

Vegetarians can add a fried egg if they prefer, cooking it in the pan last after they have made their fried bread.

If you like vegan or vegetarian versions of 'bacon' a few rashers could be included at this point too.

Relax and enjoy!

Main Meals

This section has the widest range of cooking skills and processes to learn. When you have cooked any one of these recipes a few times you could jot down on the recipe page how long it took you to make - for future reference. I have not suggested timings as they vary so much with your experience.

Main Meals

Stuffed Peppers 41

Tomato Tart 43

Lentil Chilli 45

Busy Week Baked Potatoes 47

Cottage Pie 49

Bulgar Wheat Pilaf 51

Noodle and Vegetable Stir Fry 53

Tomato Pasta 55

Baked Lemon Risotto 57

Quick chickpea Curry 59

Barbecue Skewers 61

Roast Vegetables 63

Mung Bean Casserole 65

Stuffed Peppers for three

Ingredients

 Three large red peppers

 White bread crumbs

 Pack of currants

 Capers

 Pine nuts

Olive oil

 Black olives

Mint and parsley

Utensils

kettle • chopping knife • chopping board • sieve • tablespoon • oven proof baking dish

---

Pre-heat oven 180°C or 356°F electric, 160°C or 320°F fan, gas mark 4.

Make 75g of white bread crumbs from country loaf.

Soak 30g currants in boiling water.

Toast 30g pine nuts under grill until lightly browned.

 Rinse 22g of Capers.

Chop 23g black olives.

Chop parsley and mint finely to make eight grams of herbs altogether.

Mix breadcrumbs, currants, capers, pine nuts, chopped olives and herbs to make stuffing.

 Use a scrunched up paper kitchen towel to rub a little oil onto the inside of your baking dish.

Spoon stuffing into halved red peppers and place in baking dish.

Drizzle peppers with a little olive oil and bake in oven for 45 minutes to one hour.
The peppers should be soft and tender.

Serve each person with two pepper halves and salad.

Cooking Peppers

Peppers come in a variety of shapes and sizes. The flavour of red, yellow and green peppers are similar.

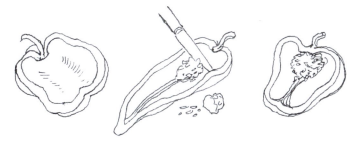

Before cooking cut the peppers in half and carefully remove the seeds and membrane. These halves can provide containers for a variety of stuffings, or can be cut into pieces or strips for vegetable dishes or salads.

Some people find raw peppers in salads indigestible, in which case you could cook the pepper pieces in hot water for 15 minutes before cooling to use when cold.

Alternatively, you could use a jar of roasted peppers in oil. Drain from the oil, pat with kitchen paper and cut into the required strips.

If you would like pepper rings, rather than strips for your salad, cut off the stem end, remove the seeds and membrane with a sharp knife and then slice across, as in the diagram.

Tomato Tart for four

Ingredients

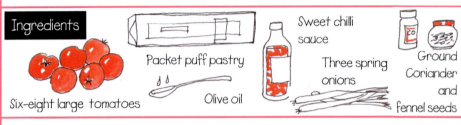

Six-eight large tomatoes • Packet puff pastry • Olive oil • Sweet chilli sauce • Three spring onions • Ground Coriander and fennel seeds

Utensils

frying pan • sharp knife • tablespoon • spatula • wooden spoon • baking tray • a wide plate

---

Cut tomatoes into firm slices – not too thin.

Add tablespoon of oil and a tablespoon of chilli sauce to warm pan.

Sprinkle in teaspoon of coriander and a heaped teaspoon of fennel seeds. Stir together gently.

Add tomato slices to pan and cook on a low heat.

Turn over carefully with the spatula to cook both sides.

Space tomatoes in pan, do not crowd together.

Cook them in batches, adding a little more oil and chilli sauce as you go.

When the tomatoes begin to soften slightly use the spatula to remove from the pan onto a wide plate and set aside.

Heat oven 200°C or 392°F electric, 180°C or 356°F fan, gas mark 6.

Unroll your pastry onto a greased baking tray.

Lightly mark out a border on the oblong pastry base. Transfer the tomatoes to inside the border, arranging neatly. Drizzle over any pan juices and the finely sliced onions.

Cook in oven for 30 minutes.

Puff Pastry Tarts

Ready-rolled puff pastry is a real time-saver in the kitchen, useful for a variety of sweet and savoury dishes. You can buy an all butter variety or those made with vegetable oil suitable for vegans.

An alternative Savoury Vegetable Tart

100g of waxy small potatoes sliced
2 leeks thinly sliced
3 tablespoons of basil pesto
Handful of cherry tomatoes halved

Handful of black olives
1 tablespoon of capers
Sprigs of basil leaves for garnish

- Preheat the oven to 200°C/392°C electric, 180°C/356°F fan, gas mark 6

- Parboil the sliced potatoes until just tender. Drain, season well and drizzle over a spoonful of olive oil and sprinkle with black pepper. Set aside.

- Cook the sliced leeks in a tablespoon of olive oil until tender, stirring now and again. Set aside.

- Lay out your pastry base with a marked border as in the recipe opposite. Use a fork to prick the base inside the border. Bake in the oven until golden brown. Remove from oven but do not turn the empty oven off yet.

- Spread two tablespoons of basil pesto over the pastry base inside the border. Cover with the potatoes and leeks.

- Top with the tomatoes, black olives and capers, and return to the oven for five minutes to heat through.

- Garnish with basil sprigs and **very** small spoonfuls of pesto.

Lentil Chilli for Four

Ingredients

One tablespoon of Olive oil

One onion

Cumin, coriander, chilli flakes (spices)

Two tins chopped tomatoes

Bouillon powder

Two tins green lentils

One tin kidney beans

Handful of fresh coriander

Utensils large saucepan • sieve • chopping knife • scissors • tin opener • one teaspoon • one dessert spoon • one wooden spoon

Chop onion finely.

Heat one tablespoon of oil in saucepan.

Add onion, cook until softened, stirring gently.

Add one teaspoon each of spices and cook for one minute.

Stir in both tins of tomatoes.

Before adding tins of lentils rinse and drain them in a sieve under the cold tap.

Cook gently for 10 minutes with one dessert spoon of bouillon powder stirred through.

Rinse and drain the kidney beans, add and heat thoroughly.

Snip coriander and stir through chilli.

Reserve a few sprigs to sprinkle on top.

Portions can be eaten with a baked potato, brown rice, lightly toasted flat breads or with slices of crusty bread and salad.

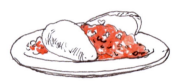

Lentils, Chillies and Onion

Lentils

Lentils are a particularly useful store cupboard ingredient. Easy to use and nutritionally beneficial, they make a versatile addition to soups, stews and salads. See page 73 for a recipe for a delicious warm winter salad.

Chillies

As this is a book for beginners I suggest that you use chilli flakes rather than fresh chillies when they are called for in a recipe. Sprinkle the chilli flakes very sparingly to begin with. You can always add more if necessary but cannot 'rescue' a recipe if you have made it much too hot. Later you can graduate to using fresh chillies.

Onions

A number of the recipes in this book call for chopped onions. There is a quick technique to remove the skin and make chopping easy.

Always use a sharp knife and a chopping board.

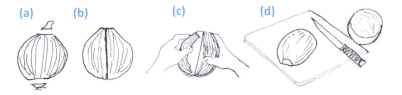

(a) Cut the top and bottom off onion.
(b) Make one cut down centre of one side.
(c) Peel back the shiny brown (or red) skin.
(d) Cut in half and place face down on board to chop into slices or chunks.

Busy Week Baked Potatoes

Ingredients

Pack of four baking potatoes Tin of baked beans Chestnut mushrooms  Jar of roasted peppers Cheese Tomatoes Olive oil Vegetable stock cube

Utensils

fork • baking tray • foil • grater
knife • chopping board • small saucepan

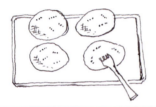

Prick potatoes all over with a fork. Place on a baking tray in a pre-heated oven and bake for one hour.
200°C or 392°F electric,
180°C or 356°F fan, gas mark 6.

Potatoes not wanted that day can be completely cooled and then wrapped in foil and put in the fridge for later in the week.

When required heat potatoes in the microwave (or oven) until hot all through, then split open and serve with a choice of fillings.

Suggested Fillings

- Baked beans and grated cheese
- Portion of Lentil Chilli (page 45)
- Tomato filling - a mixture of chopped tomatoes and peppers heated in a small saucepan in a little olive oil and herb seasoning.
- Mushroom filling - chopped chestnut mushrooms heated in vegetable stock until stock evaporated.

The addition of a salad or cooked green vegetables makes this into a main meal.

Potato with tomato filling and broccoli.

Super Quick Suppers

If you have a busy week ahead and won't have much time for cooking this is a simple solution ...

- Cook the baked potatoes at the weekend, then cool and store in the fridge wrapped in foil when completely cold.

- On a weekday evening when you come in a simple filling will take only minutes to prepare while you are reheating one of your potatoes in the microwave.

- The suggested fillings opposite are all quick to prepare. If you prefer a side-salad rather than a green vegetable choose something simple, eg thinly sliced fennel with orange segments; little gem lettuce with thinly sliced radish, spring onion and celery.

- If you prefer to cook your potato in the microwave from scratch and do not want to cook them ahead in the oven to get a crunchy flavoursome skin, you can cook one each evening while you prepare the filling, side-salad or green veg.

> To cook your potato in the microwave, rather than reheat it, pierce it a few times with a sharp knife, then place it on a microwaveable plate and cook four to six minutes on high (depending on the size of your potato). Turn the potato over and cook again on high for four to six minutes. Test to see if soft all through with a small sharp knife. Split open, season and serve with a knob of butter or vegan alternative, plus your choice of filling.

Cottage Pie for three to four

Ingredients

 Half large red onion
 Half red pepper
 Coconut cream
 Olive oil
 Three large sweet potatoes
 One large carrot
 Button mushrooms
 Tin green lentils
Thyme
Stock cube
Tomato passata
Sea salt

Utensils knife • chopping board • potato masher or fork • colander
large saucepan • large frying pan with lid • measuring jug
scales • wooden spoon

Peel potatoes and cut into even sized chunks. Place in saucepan with cold water to cover.	Bring to boil and boil for 15 minutes. Drain well. Return to pan. 	Mash potatoes thoroughly with 40ml coconut cream and salt to taste. Set aside.
	Pre-heat oven to 200°C or 392°F electric, 180°C or 356°F fan, gas mark 6. Peel, slice and chop onion. Fry gently in one tablespoon of olive oil for 7-10 minutes, stirring throughout.	Peel and dice carrot. Deseed and chop pepper. Slice 75g mushrooms. Chop thyme leaves taken off stalks.
Add all vegetables and thyme to frying pan and cook for five minutes. Add 120ml passata.	Add 175ml vegetable stock made with hot water and a stock cube. Bring to boil, then lower heat to simmer for 10 minutes.	Tip the drained and rinsed lentils into the pan. Cover with lid and simmer for 10 minutes stirring now and again.

Pile the seasoned lentil and vegetable mixture into a medium sized pie dish. Spoon the sweet potato mash on top to cover, swirling to make peaks. Cook in the pre-heated oven for 20 minutes or until crispy on top. Serve with a green vegetable. Cooking instructions on page 64.

Cottage Pie Variations

- Instead of sweet potatoes you could use ordinary potatoes for the mash topping. Season the mash with salt and pepper, and with a spoonful of butter, margarine or spread of your choice. You could also add a small spoon of Dijon or coarse grained mustard if you like.

- To vary the flavour of the filling you could add a small amount of chopped cooked parsnips and celery, together with half a tin of chopped tomatoes to the vegetable and lentil mix of the original recipe.

- When the pie is almost ready remove from the oven and grate cheese of your choice over the top. Place the pie dish under a very hot pre-heated grill for a few minutes. Watch to see that the topping is browning and not burning.

Use oven gloves or thickly folded tea towels to handle hot dishes carefully

- Individual pies can be made by piling the ingredients into several small dishes. Cook all together either to share with friends or to keep some in the fridge for later in the week. **Always cool hot dishes completely before placing in the fridge.**

Bulgar Wheat Pilaf for four

Ingredients

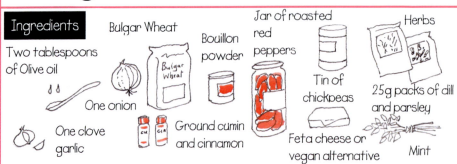

- Two tablespoons of Olive oil
- One onion
- One clove garlic
- Bulgar Wheat
- Bouillon powder
- Ground cumin and cinnamon
- Jar of roasted red peppers
- Tin of chickpeas
- Feta cheese or vegan alternative
- Herbs
- 25g packs of dill and parsley
- Mint

Utensils

large saucepan • table spoon • dessert spoon • sieve • fork • wooden spoon • kitchen scissors • chopping knife

---

Heat the oil in the saucepan and cook the finely chopped onion until golden, stirring frequently.

Add the chopped garlic clove.

Add 175g of bulgar wheat and one teaspoon each of cumin and cinnamon.

Stir one dessert spoon of bouillon powder into 300ml of hot water to make vegetable stock.

Pour onto wheat in pan and bring to the boil.

Cover the pan and turn down the heat.

Cook gently until all liquid absorbed.

Add the drained chickpeas.

Take 200g of peppers from jar, drain and chop roughly. Add to the pan. DO NOT STIR. LEAVE TO REST FOR 15 MINUTES WITH THE LID ON. Uncover and fluff up the pilaf with a fork.

Chop 25g packs of dill and parsley and add a handful of chopped mint. Fold the herbs gently into the pilaf and season to taste. Crumble 200g of Feta cheese or vegan alternative on top.

Serve warm or cold

New Grains

Bulgar wheat is one of the healthy new grains that are becoming widely used today. It is a whole-grain made from cracked wheat and is packed with vitamins, minerals and fibre. It has slightly fewer calories than many other whole grains.

Couscous is composed of grains of semolina with a fine wheat-flour coating. It is the ultimate grain for speed cooking. As it can be bland it is usually combined with flavoursome ingredients in recipes. See pages 56 and 72.

Quinoa (pronounced keen-wah) looks like couscous but is actually a fruit seed which contains complete protein and lots of minerals which makes it ideal for vegetarians and vegans. It is a powerhouse of a grain, often used in vegetable dishes and stuffings. See page 74.

Noodle & Vegetable Stir-fry for one

Ingredients

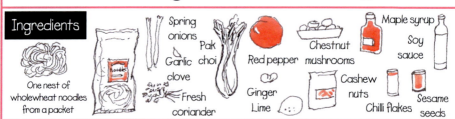

One nest of wholewheat noodles from a packet • Spring onions • Pak choi • Garlic clove • Fresh coriander • Red pepper • Chestnut mushrooms • Ginger • Lime • Maple syrup • Soy sauce • Cashew nuts • Chilli flakes • Sesame seeds

Utensils

saucepan • colander • knife • chopping board • wok • small bowl • lemon squeezer • teaspoon • dessertspoon

---

Cook noodles in saucepan according to instructions on the packet. Drain, rinse and set aside in colander.

Peel and finely chop the garlic clove and peel and chop a half inch piece of ginger. Chop two spring onions. Cut 40g of mushrooms into small chunks.

Cut the pak choi into quarters and finely chop one quarter, storing remains in fridge. Chop half deseeded red pepper.

Add one tablespoon of oil to the wok and heat until the pan is really hot. Add garlic, ginger and half teaspoon flakes and the spring onions. Cook, stirring for two minutes.

Add the chopped mushrooms and cook for one minute. Into a small bowl pour one dessertspoon of soy sauce, one desert spoon of maple syrup and the juice of half a lime.

Add the contents of half the bowl to the pan, along with the chopped red pepper and the chopped pak choi, and cook together for two minutes. Add the drained noodles and the rest of the sauce from the bowl and cook for a further two to three minutes.

Remove from the heat and transfer to your serving bowl. Top with a sprinkling of sesame seeds, some toasted cashew nuts, and snipped fresh coriander. Add a <u>few</u> more chilli flakes if liked.

Stir-frying

Stir-frying is a very quick method of cooking. The actual cooking takes only minutes but the preparation first is more time-consuming.

As in the recipe opposite all the chopping and slicing of ingredients must be done in advance, and any sauces or extras, ready to go.

A wok is invaluable for this type of cooking, although you could use a large saucepan if necessary. The wok's high sides control any spitting caused by the high heat.

A very simple stir-fry vegetable dish, which requires very little vegetable preparation, is as follows:

Pak Choi and Sugar Snap Stir-fry

225 grams of pak choi, root trimmed and sliced into quarters
200 grams sugar snap peas halved length-wise.

Place one tablespoon of sunflower oil in a wok over a high heat. Add the vegetables and stir-fry for three to four minutes until the vegetables soften.

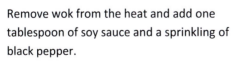

Remove wok from the heat and add one tablespoon of soy sauce and a sprinkling of black pepper.

Serve at once as a side dish.

Tomato Pasta for two

Ingredients

Olive oil • Whole wheat penne pasta Half a red onion • Two garlic cloves • Sea salt •   Chilli flakes • Tin chopped tomatoes • Black olives

Utensils two saucepans • knife • chopping board • wooden spoon • one tablespoon • colander

In first saucepan add 150 grams of penne pasta to boiling water. Cook according to packet instructions. Drain and set aside back in saucepan.	While pasta is cooking chop half a large red onion and two garlic cloves. 	Add one tablespoon olive oil to the second saucepan and add the chopped onion and garlic, a teaspoon of chilli flakes and a good pinch of salt. Stir together.
Cook gently until the onion softens, stirring now and again.	Slice 20g of black olives from the jar.	Add sliced olives and the tinned tomatoes and simmer for 20 minutes. Add one tablespoon of water.
The pasta sauce will Thicken as the ingredients simmer and will reduce in volume. Add the sauce to the drained pasta and heat together stirring gently.	 Grate over a little parmigiana or vegan equivalent.	

Tips for cooking dried pasta shapes

When you have put the pasta into a large saucepan of boiling water a little oil or butter can be added to prevent the pasta sticking together while cooking. As the pasta cooks it will increase in size. It is best not to cover the pan to avoid water boiling over.

Cook the pasta until it is 'al dente' - still with a little firmness to it - not completely soft and floppy. Test to see if it is ready by removing a piece of pasta from the pan, allow to cool a little and test it with your teeth. Approximate cooking time 10-12 minutes, wholemeal shapes a little longer - 15 minutes.

Make your sauce while the pasta is cooking so that, as far as possible, they are ready together. When the pasta is cooked drain in a colander, and then put back in the hot pan. Any sauces can be poured on top or stirred through.

Serve the pasta on hot plates that you have warmed under the grill or in the oven.

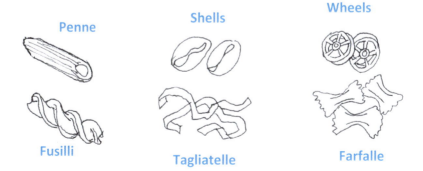

Penne

Shells

Wheels

Fusilli

Tagliatelle

Farfalle

Baked Lemon Risotto for four

Ingredients

Butter, margarine or vegan spread

One large onion

One lemon

Two garlic cloves

Arborio risotto rice

Vegan stock cubes

Parmesan cheese or vegan alternative

Utensils large saucepan • knife • chopping board • wooden spoon • graters • baking dish • lemon squeezer • kitchen foil • measuring jug

Preheat oven 180°C or 356°F electric, 160°C or 320°F fan, gas mark 4.

Take a piece of foil and make a rough lid for your baking dish. Remove lid and set aside for later.

Grate zest from half a lemon.

Squeeze juice from half a lemon.

Chop onion and garlic finely. Melt 30g butter or vegan spread in large saucepan and cook onion and garlic for five minutes on a low heat.

Add the lemon juice and zest together with 275g risotto rice. Mix together thoroughly.

Add 875ml hot stock made with stock cubes. Taste for saltiness.

Season lightly and bring risotto to the boil. When it starts to bubble pour it carefully into your large baking dish.

Bake for 12 minutes in the pre-heated oven. Then open the oven door and stir the risotto gently with wooden spoon. Carefully drop the foil lid you made earlier over the dish and bake for another eight to ten minutes. Grate over a little cheese of choice.

Serve with baked mushrooms (page 22) and a green vegetable.
To use any leftovers see opposite page.

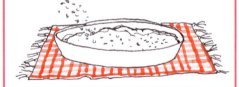

Rice

For this baked risotto we are using Italian Arborio rice which is necessary for any type of risotto as it cooks to a creamy texture.

Brown basmati rice is particularly nourishing and used in many vegetarian and vegan recipes. It is rich in B vitamins and has well documented health benefits.

Wild rice (actually a grass seed) is the most expensive.

Pudding rice is white, a short, plump rice for sweet dishes.

Long grain white rice is usually for savoury dishes.

If you are in a hurry it can be useful to buy pre-cooked rice in a pouch to reheat on the cooker or to microwave in a couple of minutes (not for the recipe opposite).

Arancini

To use left-over risotto. Cool the risotto. If at all sloppy drain in a sieve and then refrigerate for not more than two days until ready to use.

Take a tablespoon of rice and shape into a little patty. Push a couple of cubes of cheese into the centre, together with a little dollop of pesto from a jar. Then put more rice on top, moulding the rice to completely enclose the cheese. Repeat making more patties. Dust each patty with flour, then dip in beaten egg and finally roll in fine breadcrumbs. Fry patties gently until golden brown and cooked all through. Eat with salad or a green vegetable.

Quick Chickpea Curry for two

Ingredients

- Olive oil
- Two cloves garlic
- Piece of ginger
- Half onion
- Tin of chickpeas
- Small tin chopped tomatoes
- Packet of Naan breads
- Coriander
- Tomato puree
- Ground cinnamon, curry powder, cumin seeds
- Pouch of pre-baked long grain rice

Utensils
one large saucepan • wooden spoon • sieve • kitchen scissors

Chop onion and garlic finely and grate two teaspoons ginger. Add these to a tablespoon of olive oil and heat for two minutes in saucepan, stirring gently until garlic and ginger are softened.

Add: one teaspoon of ground cinnamon, one tablespoon of curry powder, one teaspoon of cumin seeds, and cook gently, still stirring frequently.

Drain and rinse chickpeas

Add chickpeas, tin of tomatoes and two tablespoons tomato puree to saucepan.

Cook contents of saucepan for ten minutes over a medium to high heat so that the liquid is bubbling gently. Season to taste.
Snip some coriander to sprinkle over curry.

Serve curry with warmed Naan breads and the rice cooked according to pouch instructions.

Optional extra:
Make a small bowl of raita (finely diced cucumber stirred through plain yoghurt) to spoon on top of your curry.

Curries

There are so many and varied types of curry that there have been whole recipe books devoted to them.

On the opposite page I have started you off with a very simple, quick 'store cupboard ingredients' version.

If, later, you want to cook a more complex curry the recipe below is very quick to cook, once you have all the ingredients collected together. Serve with brown rice.

Thai Vegetable Curry for 2-3

200ml can coconut milk
¼ teaspoon ground coriander
¼ teaspoon ground cumin
1 Kaffir lime leaf
1cm piece fresh ginger peeled and sliced
1 stalk lemongrass
1 tablespoon of chopped fresh coriander
50g sugar-snap peas

½ a small red pepper sliced
½ a small yellow pepper sliced
50g baby corn halved lengthwise
½ aubergine chopped
2 courgettes chopped
1 spring onion finely sliced
Small handful bean sprouts
Fresh basil leaves

- Heat the coconut milk in a wok until boiling. Then add the spices, lime leaf, ginger, lemongrass and fresh coriander. Cook two to three minutes on high heat. Remove lime leaf and lemongrass stalk.

- Add the peas, peppers, baby corn, aubergine and courgette and cook for three to four minutes until vegetables are just done.

- Sprinkle on the spring onion, bean sprouts and basil and serve straight from the wok with brown rice.

Barbecue Skewers

Ingredients

Pack of vegetarian or vegan sausages

Jar of roasted peppers in oil

Two red onions

Tin of new potatoes

Sweet chilli sauce or jam

Utensils pastry brush • kitchen paper • knife • eight wooden skewers • chopping board

Soak the wooden skewers in warm water before starting.	Cut the sausages into roughly even sized chunks.	
Cut onions into wedges.	Take potatoes from the tin. Drain and pat dry with kitchen paper.	Take 300g of peppers from jar and set aside. Mix two tablespoons of oil from the jar with two tablespoons of sweet chilli sauce or jam to make a glaze.
Thread onions, peppers, potatoes and sausage chunks onto skewers. Peppers can be folded over to go onto skewers. 	Brush skewers thoroughly on all sides with the chilli/oil glaze. Should make between six to eight skewers in all.	Cook on the barbecue or under a hot grill, turning frequently for about 10 minutes until cooked. Test carefully to see they are cooked all through before serving.

Vegetarian and Vegan Sausages

Some people find vegetarian and vegan sausages rather bland, but you may be able to find some you enjoy. They are useful in well-flavoured dishes.

In the recipe opposite, brushing the pieces of sausage with a chilli oil glaze helps to pep up the flavour.

Another useful idea is to make a rich onion gravy to go with the traditional meal of sausage and mashed potato. Start in good time because it takes about an hour to make.

Onion Gravy

- Thinly slice a large red onion - or two small ones - and cook in a spoonful of olive oil and a spoonful of butter or vegan spread for 20 minutes on a low heat stirring frequently.
- Season well with salt and pepper, and a sprinkle of dried thyme.
- Stir a flat dessertspoon of plain flour into the mix until it is all absorbed.
- Gradually add 300ml of vegetable stock, stirring as you go.
- Bring to the boil.
- Once boiled then turn down heat and cook very gently on a low heat for a further 20 minutes.
- Stir in a large spoonful of red currant jelly (optional) and serve.

Roast Vegetables

Ingredients

Carrots
Parsnips
Potatoes
Celeriac
Red onions
Half a butternut squash
Olive Oil
Mixed herbs

Utensils
knife • chopping board • large baking tray • tablespoon

Pre-heat oven 200°C or 392°F electric, 180°C or 356°F fan, gas mark 6.	Peel the vegetables, the amount dictated by the number you are catering for. Cut into equal sized medium chunks.	Spread out on a large baking tray with three tablespoons of olive oil or rape seed oil. Toss well together.
Mix with sea salt, mixed herbs and pepper sprinkled over.		Roast for 30-60 minutes, stirring well half way through cooking time. Vegetables are ready when tender and beginning to brown a little.

Vegetarian or vegan sausages could be cooked alongside the vegetables on the baking tray, or grilled separately and added at the finish, if you wish.

A different mix of vegetables goes very well with cooked pasta.

½ red onion cut into wedges
½ chopped red pepper
½ large tomato chopped
½ courgette sliced thickly
½ aubergine chopped

Place on the baking tray with oil and seasoning as above.

When roasted, chop veg smaller and stir through pasta together with a tablespoon of tomato pesto.

Cooking Vegetables

- Root vegetables, potatoes, beetroot and squash can all be roasted, baked or boiled.
- Onions and leeks add their flavours to a great variety of recipes and cooking methods.

Cooking Green Vegetables

Vegetable	Preparation
Kale Cabbage	Chop finely
Sprouts	Slice off the base and remove a few outer leaves
Cauliflower Broccoli Sprouting broccoli	Cut into small florets
Runner beans French beans	Cut into short even sized lengths
Peas Broad beans	Remove from pods unless frozen
Spinach	Remove any hard centre stalks

After preparation green vegetables are placed in a saucepan of lightly salted boiling water and cooked for 10-20 minutes. Test with a fork or by tasting to see if they are ready. You want them to retain a **slight** crispness. **Do NOT overcook** or they lose colour and goodness. The water used for cooking greens retains nutrients and can be drunk or used in soups and stews.

Spinach is cooked differently from all the other greens. When you have prepared and washed it put it in a large saucepan with only a spoonful of water, over a moderate heat. It will wilt down in a few minutes of stirring

Drain all green vegetables thoroughly in a sieve or colander before serving. Steaming green vegetables instead of boiling them retains all their vitamin content. An inexpensive bamboo steamer would be useful here. Look online for stockists.

Mung Bean Casserole for three or four

Ingredients

 Pack of mung beans

 Vegetable stock cube

 Turmeric powder

 Ground cumin

 Fresh coriander

 Two carrots

Two heads of chicory

 One onion

 Bean sprouts

 Small bunch of radishes

Utensils

teaspoon • tablespoon • sieve • knife • chopping board measuring jug

---

Soak 250g mung beans in cold water for six hours or overnight.

Drain the beans and rinse well.

Bring 750ml of water to the boil. Add drained beans and the crumbled stock cube, ½ teaspoon turmeric, ½ teaspoon cumin. Lower heat and simmer for 30 minutes.

Chop the onion and carrots finely, add to the pan with chopped coriander and simmer for a further 15 minutes.

Separate the leaves of chicory.

Arrange the chicory leaves round the edge of a deep bowl and spoon in the drained bean mix. Garnish with sliced radishes and bean sprouts.

Serve with brown rice and a colourful salad. The beans and rice combined together make a complete protein.

Beans and Nutrition

When beans and grains are eaten together they make a very valuable complete protein that the body can absorb easily, particularly valuable for vegetarians and vegans, who are not getting protein from animal products. Some of the many ways beans and grains can be combined: bean casseroles with brown rice, bean salads with couscous, bean soups eaten with oatcakes, broad beans and vegetables with risotto rice, beans on toast, etc.
A delicious simple broth that combines beans and grains is:

Bean and Barley Broth – enough for two servings

750ml of vegetable stock
50g pearl barley
Few leaves of fresh cabbage, Kale or greens
1 medium carrot

100g frozen peas or petit pois
400g tin of cannellini beans
Sea salt and pepper
Olive oil

- Bring stock to boil.
- Add rinsed and drained pearl barley, reduce heat and simmer until tender - 30-40 minutes.
- Dice carrots and boil separately for 10 minutes.
- Shred and chop greens finely.
- Add drained carrots, greens, peas and beans to pan, simmer five minutes.
- Season and serve adding a trickle of olive oil on top.

As in the recipe opposite, dried beans often need pre-soaking and pre-cooking. This preparation is easy and simple to do but is time-consuming, so build it into the timing of your menu-planning.

Fortunately it is possible to find tins of many kinds of beans which are pre-cooked and ready to be drained, rinsed and used immediately as in this recipe using cannellini beans in Bean and Barley Broth.

Salads

There are a surprising number of salad ingredients and innumerable ways of combining them.

I have chosen a few seasonal salads to introduce some more unusual food combinations.

Salads

Spring Dandelion and Apple Salad................ 69

Fennel and Citrus Summer Salad.................. 71

Rice, Shallot and Beetroot Winter Salad 73

Spring Dandelion + Apple Salad for one

Ingredients

Handful of dandelion leaves • Salt • Honey or maple syrup • Sweet apple • Raisins • Lemon • Apple cider vinegar • Vegan or dairy butter • Fennel seeds

Utensils kitchen scissors • small saucepan • one tablespoon • one teaspoon • knife and chopping board

Wash dandelion leaves thoroughly and snip into short narrow ribbons.

Dice the apple.

Toss leaves and apple together in bowl.

Warm one tablespoon of butter in a small pan over a low heat.

Add a dessertspoon of fennel seeds.

Turn up the heat a little and stir gently for a while until seeds start to brown.

Add 40 grams of raisins, one teaspoon of cider vinegar and one dessertspoon of honey or syrup and simmer for five minutes.

Drizzle warm raisins and seeds over leaves and apple.

Toss the salad with one teaspoon lemon juice and ½ teaspoon salt. Serve as a side dish or with crusty bread and butter with cheese or houmous.

This Spring salad is an example of recipes in the seasonal eating programme mentioned on page 90.

Eating Dandelion Leaves

The recipe opposite is a Spring recipe when the dandelion leaves are young and tender. Old leaves will be leathery and bitter.

A shows a mature dandelion plant with buds, a flower and its distinctive fluffy white seed-head. In the springtime you are more likely to find B, just a rosette of serrated leaves without much in the way of flowers.

Never pick dandelions from the side of the road where they can be polluted by traffic fumes. Look for the leaves in parks and gardens or in the countryside away from traffic and wash them well before use.

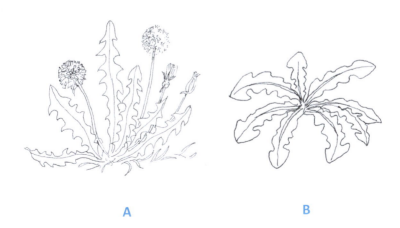

A   B

Fennel and Citrus — Summer Salad for one

Ingredients

Two satsumas or clementines

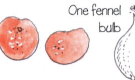

One fennel bulb

Watercress — Olive oil

Utensils

sharp serrated knife • chopping board • lemon squeezer
paper kitchen towels • small screw topped jar

If the outer leaves of the bulb are coarse then shave them thinly.

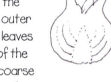

Cut bulb in half.

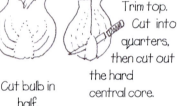

Trim top. Cut into quarters, then cut out the hard central core.

Trim one quarter into wafer thin slices with sharp knife. Store rest in fridge.

Peel one satsuma.

Cut carefully into thin slices.

To make this salad for more than one just increase ingredients.

Break the watercress into small sprigs, removing any long stalks.

Wash thoroughly and pat dry with paper towel.

Add juice of the second satsuma to a teaspoon of olive oil and a very little sea salt.

Put into a small screw-topped jar and shake vigorously to make a citrus dressing.

Arrange your salad.

Pour over some citrus dressing. Store surplus in jar in fridge.

Summer Salads

There is an increasing tendency to include fruit in summer salads today. See the watermelon, radish, celery and tomato salad on page 86.

Two other variations including fruit are:

Pear, Goat's Cheese, Pecan Nuts and Lettuce Summer Salad

Use the inner leaves of a Little Gem lettuce to line your plate. Top with small chunks of goat's cheese or vegan alternative and a sprinkling of pecan nuts, or walnut halves. Arrange thin slices of juicy ripe pear in a circle on top. Use a light dressing of your choice.

Fruity Couscous Summer Salad with Mango

Put 90g couscous into a heat proof bowl and just cover with boiling water. Give it a stir and then cover the bowl with a plate. Set aside for ten minutes, until all the water has been absorbed. Fluff up with a fork. Pour the juice of half a lemon over the couscous and add one teaspoon of finely chopped fresh ginger, half a teaspoon of chilli flakes and two tablespoons EACH of chopped coriander, mint and parsley. Stir together and season well. Allow to cool completely. Top the herby couscous with chunks of ripe fresh mango.

You could choose instead from a selection of usual salad ingredients if you prefer: watercress, lettuce, tomatoes, cucumber, radish, celery, spring onions, avocado, asparagus and so on. Fruit is not mandatory!

Rice, Shallot & Beetroot   Winter Salad for four

Ingredients

One pouch of ready cooked long grain and wild rice

Bouillon powder

Four shallots

Olive oil
One lemon

Pack of four cooked beetroot

Mint, chives, parsley

Utensils
one medium and one small saucepan • chopping knife • teaspoon
chopping board • baking tray • lemon squeezer • sieve

Pre-heat oven 200°C or 392°F electric, 180°C or 356°F fan, gas mark 6.	Prepare the shallots. Peel and halve.  	
Place shallots in the medium saucepan. Cover with water and bring to the boil. Boil for two minutes, remove from heat, drain and cool.	Lightly grease a baking tray. Place the drained shallots on the tray, drizzle with oil and roast for five minutes, then allow to cool.	Place 200 grams of rice from the pouch in the small saucepan. Add water just to cover, with a heaped teaspoon of bouillon powder. Simmer gently for five minutes.
Drain the rice and allow to cool. Squeeze the juice from the lemon. Chop two tablespoons EACH from the mint, chives and parsley.	 Dice beetroot and mix cooled rice with the beetroot, lemon juice and chopped herbs. Mix together with the shallots roughly chopped.	 This vibrant salad would go well with any number of vegan or vegetarian meals. To serve warm, heat the rice from the pouch just before you stir it into all the other ingredients, having drained it first.

Winter Salads

Using grains and pulses in winter salads adds to their comforting appeal in the colder months as in the salad opposite.

Another alternative is:

Quinoa Supper Salad

Rinse 100g of quinoa in several changes of cold water. Put in a saucepan with a pinch of salt and cover with plenty of cold water. Bring to the boil, reduce heat and simmer for about 12 minutes. Tip into a sieve, drain and set aside.

In a large saucepan melt a knob of butter or vegan spread with a tablespoon of olive or rapeseed oil and place over a medium heat. Add 400g of thinly sliced courgettes, a large sliced and chopped onion and one big garlic clove finely chopped. Sprinkle with dried or fresh thyme leaves. Cook gently for 20-25 minutes, stirring now and again.

Add the drained quinoa, a handful of roughly chopped parsley, and the juice of half a lemon. Season well and top with 30g pine nuts lightly toasted.

A useful pulse salad is:

Warm Red Lentil Salad

Rinse and drain 100g of red lentils and place in a medium saucepan. Add two peeled and chopped shallots, a chopped garlic clove, a teaspoon of chopped fresh ginger and two teaspoons of bouillon powder. Cover with cold water, bring to the boil, then lower heat and simmer for 10-15 minutes; stirring now and again. Cool a little, drain thoroughly and pile onto plates, spread with salad leaves. Garnish with chopped coriander or mint with lime wedges to squeeze over.

Desserts

Desserts are particularly appealing when served on attractive platters, bowls and dishes, or in pretty glasses and cups.

I hope that when you get to the Celebration Trifle, the last recipe in the book, you will make it to celebrate just how far you have come since page 1.

Desserts

Simple Apple Crumble 77

Baked Nectarines 79

Fruit Jellies 81

Fruit Salads 83

Watermelon Treats 85

Celebration Trifle 87

Simple Apple Crumble for four

Ingredients

Three large Bramley apples

Caster sugar

Plain flour

Ground cinnamon

Butter or vegan marg

Dairy/vegan ice cream

Utensils knife • chopping board • mixing bowl • ice cream scoop or large spoon

Preheat oven 180°C or 356°F electric, 160°C or 320°F fan, gas mark 4.

Add 280g flour and 100g of sugar into bowl.

Add 90g of butter or marg and rub together with finger tips until like breadcrumbs.

Set crumble mix aside.

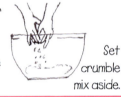

Cut each apple into half and then into segments.

Peel segments.

Cut out cores.

Chop segments into chunks.

Place the apple chunks and a pinch of cinnamon in a shallow greased baking dish. Sprinkle with a little sugar.

Scatter crumble mix over apples and bake for 35-40 minutes until the top is golden and juice bubbles up around the edges.

Crumble mix variations:
- Add a spoonful of porridge oats for an extra crunchy topping
- Use 200g flour and 50g ground almonds for a different flavour
- Add chopped hazel nuts to topping

Apple variation:
- Add a large spoonful of blackberries to the apples

Serve with a scoop of dairy or vegan ice cream.

Fruit Crumbles

Apple Crumble has long been popular, but there are other fruit crumbles to try:

Three different fillings:

- **Rhubarb** 750g of rhubarb cut into short chunks. Add 120g of sugar, the grated zest of a small orange and the juice of half an orange.

- **Gooseberry** 750g of gooseberries which have been topped and tailed (snip off tops and tails with scissors). Stew the gooseberries in a little water with 140g of sugar until soft before adding to baking dish.

- **Plum** 750g of plums, halved and stoned. Stew the plums in 70g of sugar and a little water before adding to baking dish.

A variety of dairy or vegan creams, custards or ice cream can accompany these crumbles.

Making the crumble topping:

When 'rubbing in' fat to flour remember a few tips:

- Use fat cool from the fridge and cut into dice-sized or small pieces.

- Pick up a small handful of fat and flour in each hand and rub together with your finger-tips, before letting the crumbs fall into the bowl. Do this well above the bowl to 'let air into the mixture'. Repeat until all the fat has been rubbed in.

Baked Nectarines for four

Ingredients

Four ripe nectarines

One lime

Piece of fresh ginger

Golden castor sugar

Utensils knife • spoon • teaspoon • grater • measuring jug small bowl • lemon squeezer • scales

Preheat oven 200°C or 392°F electric, 180°C or 356°F fan, gas mark 6.

Halve nectarines and remove stones.

Peel approx. 1½cm square of ginger root with a teaspoon.

Then grate coarsely.

Squeeze the juice from each of the lime halves.

Mix together the lime juice, 175g sugar and the grated ginger to make a paste.

Top each nectarine half with a spoonful of the ginger and sugar mix.

Place nectarine halves carefully on an oven-proof dish or tray. Pour 70ml of cold water into the tray around the nectarines. Lift carefully into pre-heated oven keeping the baking tray level.

Bake 30-40 minutes depending on ripeness of fruit. Test with a fork to see that the nectarines are soft all through.

Best served cold with crème fraiche, soya yoghurt or vegan ice cream.

Baked Fruits

- Quite a number of fruits can be baked in this way. Peaches and plums make an alternative to nectarines; cooked with sugar and ginger, or sugar and a few drops of vanilla essence.

- Slices or wedges of fresh pineapple or halved bananas don't need ginger, just a topping of sugar and a little water in the baking dish - and perhaps a dash of rum, or rum essence, if you like it.

- You can store any unused ginger wrapped tightly in foil in the fridge for a week or so. Halves of lime or lemon can be stored in this way too.

- Replace golden caster sugar with a dark brown muscovado sugar for all these baked fruits to make a delicious difference.

- To halve ripe stoned fruits such as nectarines, peaches and plums for baking follow the diagrams below. If the fruits are not ripe they will not twist apart, so you could slice them instead before cooking.

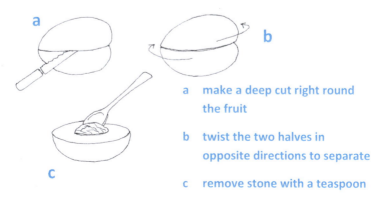

a   make a deep cut right round the fruit

b   twist the two halves in opposite directions to separate

c   remove stone with a teaspoon

Fruit Jellies for four to six

Ingredients

 Sachet of gelatine-free jelly crystals

 Water

 Small punnet raspberries

 Large banana

Dairy or vegan cream

Utensils measuring jug • knife • large spoon • kettle

Place crystals in measuring jug and make up to 600ml with boiling water.

Stir until crystals dissolve completely. Allow to cool a while then pour into serving bowl.

Slice banana thinly and add to bowl. The slices will float on top.

Allow to cool and then refrigerate to set which will take at least one hour.

Put spoonfuls of set jelly into individual dishes or glasses.

Decorate with fresh raspberries and a trickle of dairy or vegan cream.

You could select different colours and flavours of jelly and different fruits.
- Yellow or lime green jelly with slices of pear
- Deep red jelly with tinned black cherries
- Orange jelly with segments of satsumas and so on.

*Do not add fresh pineapple, kiwi fruit or papaya to the liquid jelly as they will prevent setting. These fruits could be used to garnish set jellies.

Serving Jellies

It is not always necessary to have matching glasses or bowls for serving jellies or trifles.

Charity shops often have inexpensive odds and ends of china and glass which make pretty serving dishes, especially if you visit several shops to see what you can find.

Two Fruit Salads

Ingredients

Ripe pear Small punnet raspberries Small cluster red or black seedless grapes Tin black cherries Small ripe banana Pouring cream or vegan alternative

Utensils
small sharp knife • chopping board • paper kitchen towel • dessert spoon

Wash and peel pear and cut into quarters. Core quarters, and cut into small slices. Wash grapes and pat dry with kitchen paper, then halve. Peel and slice banana and open tin of cherries.

①

For two servings share fruit between two dishes. Use all the pear slices and banana. Put a dessertspoon each of raspberries and cherries on each plate and finish with the grapes. Spoon over a little juice from the cherry tin and a trickle of cream.

Place any surplus cherries in a non-metallic container and store in fridge. They could be used on porridge, in overnight oats or to garnish fruit jellies.

Tropical Fruit Salad Summer Special ②

A selection of thinly sliced tropical fruits to share makes a treat on a hot summer day.
Select from pineapple, mango, papaya, guava, figs and kiwi fruit. Peel fruit carefully and cut into thin neat slices.

Arrange the slices on a large platter.
Keep cool in the fridge if possible or stand the platter over a dish of ice cubes, until ready to serve.

Fruit

Fruit is a wonderful resource for vegetarians and vegans being packed with vitamins, minerals and nutrients. It is an essential part of your 'five-a-day', EVERY day.

- Most fruit does not need to be cooked, making it useful for snacks, lunchboxes, picnics and so on, and makes a perfect dessert after a meal. Many fruits are also useful for delicious pies, puddings and preserves, and there are countless recipes for stewed and baked fruits.

- Fruit grown locally on allotments, in gardens or available at local markets is not only usually fresher, but is best at particular seasons, eg strawberries in June. Seasonal fruit and vegetables are particularly recommended by the seasonal eating programme mentioned on page 90.

- Store fresh soft fruits in the fridge if possible. Frozen fruit, such as a pack of mixed berries, still retains its valuable nutrients and is useful in winter. Thaw out completely before using.

- Always make sure your fresh fruit is ripe before eating. To ripen unripe fruit put it in a paper bag with a ripe banana for a day or two in a dark cupboard, or ripen it on a sunny window ledge until ready.

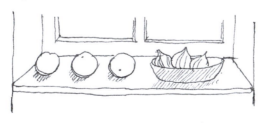

Watermelon Treats

Ingredients

One large water melon or two small ones

Pack of soft dairy or soft vegan cheese

Tub of thick dairy or vegan yoghurt

One lime

Mix of ripe soft fruits and berries

Kiwi fruit

Utensils

large mixing bowl • one large spoon • one teaspoon knife • chopping board • kitchen paper • grater

Cut four large slices from the centre of the water melon about 1½ cm thick.

Pat slices dry with kitchen paper.

Tip 200g of soft cheese and 50g of yoghurt into bowl and mix thoroughly. Cover and chill in fridge for 10 minutes.

Grate the zest from the lime.

Cut each of your large slices into segments. Use a small teaspoon to gently remove any seeds.

Spread each segment with the cheese and yoghurt mix. Slice the soft fruits into small pieces and arrange on top of each segment. Add berries and sprinkle lime zest over. Makes ten or more slices.

The water melon flesh from the unused end pieces can be used in salads (opposite page).

Watermelon Salads

The watermelon in the unused 'ends' of the melon from the recipe opposite can be used in salads. Remove the hard outer peel and chop the flesh into small pieces.

Fruit Salads

Small cubes of watermelon give a welcome freshness to a mix of fruits for a dessert.

A Savoury Salad

Mix small cubes of watermelon with halved cherry tomatoes and some thinly sliced celery and radishes. Add a spoonful of salad dressing of your choice and mix gently together. Top with chopped mint or parsley.

Celebration Trifle for six

Ingredients

 Tub of pomegranate seeds

Punnet blueberries

 Amaretti biscuits

 Pistachio nuts

 Elderflower cordial

 Dairy custard and double cream or vegan alternatives

Utensils
chopping knife • large spoon • whisk • bowl • plastic bag measuring jug

---

Crush 100 grams of amaretti biscuits in a sealed plastic bag.

Whip 400ml double cream until it will stand in Peaks.

⭐ See Below.

Chop 25 grams pistachio nuts.

You can use one large trifle bowl or six small glasses.

Layer up the ingredients starting from the Bottom.

5 Top with chopped nuts and pomegranate seeds
4 400ml whipped cream
3 500 gram carton of vanilla custard
2 Punnet of blueberries
1 Amaretti biscuits drizzled with sweet elderflower cordial

Keep custards and creams chilled in the fridge.

Layer up at the last minute.

If necessary to make in advance store in fridge if possible.

 Vegans may find vegan whipped cream in a spray can is a good substitute.

Look on line for a wide range of vegan 'custards' and 'creams', and stockists, or explore your local supermarket.

Trifle Variations

Once you have noted the rough proportions used in making a trifle there is no need for too much measuring of ingredients.

Each time you want a base of crumbled biscuits, sponge cake or sponge fingers drizzled with a small amount of flavoursome liquid, eg elderflower cordial, ginger syrup, fruit juice and so on. Then you add layers of fruit of choice, custard and cream, finishing with a garnish on top.

You can make a bowlful to share or small individual portions.

A luxury version: Apricot and ginger

Bottom layer: crumbled ginger biscuits drizzled in ginger syrup from a jar of ginger in syrup; then layers of sliced apricots (either fresh sliced apricots cooked previously in a little sugar and water or tinned ones); layers of custard and cream topped with small pieces of chopped ginger from the jar and a few snips of apricot.

A basic version: Apple and sultana

Make a base of crumbled sponge cake or sponge fingers. Top with layers of custard, cream and stewed apple (slices of peeled Bramley apple and a spoonful of sultanas stewed with sugar and a little water in a saucepan until soft). Cool completely before using. Garnish with a few chopped nuts.

Sources of Recipes

Few of these vegan and vegetarian recipes are completely original. Many have been given me by friends and I have developed a few myself. Others have been adapted from recipes I have come across in newspapers, magazines and cookery books.

As you progress, and move on from this very basic starter book, you will find a truly amazing range of recipes in magazines and books catering for vegetarians and vegans.

Some cookery writers I would recommend include:

- **Hugh Fearnley-Whittingstall** for imaginative vegetarian recipes
- **Aine Carlin** for delicious vegan recipes
- **David and Stephen Flynn** for a healthy plant-based lifestyle
- **Gillian McKeith** for nutritional information on ingredients

There are countless others and no doubt you will discover your own favourites.

Another interesting author is John Douillard. Some of his American recipes have been put on-line by Emma Frisch. His whole healthy eating programme is based on seasonal eating and contains many vegetarian and vegan options. One of his recipes has been adapted for this book on page 69.

As you progress you will probably invent or adapt your own recipes and realise that, as you become experienced, you don't always have to follow each ingredient choice exactly. Sometimes you can add, leave out or change ingredients to your own taste.

I hope this little book will have started you off on cooking your own healthy, inexpensive and enjoyable recipes

Good luck ... Happy Eating

Index Tips

To find a particular recipe consult the comprehensive Contents pages (pages 1 and 2) at the beginning of the book.

Look under the headings:

SOUPS

SNACKS

BREAKFASTS

MAIN MEALS

SALADS

DESSERTS

to locate your recipe

A

Agave syrup	iv
Apple crumble	77
Apple slices	34
Apple and dandelion salad	69
Apple and sultana trifle	88
Apricot and ginger trifle	88
Arancini	58
Avocado and tomato bruschetta	26

B

Baked beans	27, 35, 47
Baked fruits	80
Baked lemon risotto	57
Baked nectarines	79
Baked potatoes	47, 48
Barbecue skewers	61
Bean and barley broth	66
Beans and nutrition	66
Beetroot rice and shallot salad	73
Black olives	41, 44, 55
Blender	18
Breakfast fruit	34

Brunch	38
Bruschetta	26
Bulgar wheat	51, 52

C

Cabbage preparation	64
Cashew nuts	53
Celeriac	63
Chicory	65
Chickpea curry	59
Chilli flakes	46
Coconut cream	49
Coconut milk	19
Containers	11
Cottage pie	49, 50
Courgette bruschetta	26
Cous-Cous	52, 56, 72

D

Dandelion and apple salad	69
Dairy products	iv
Dedication	iii

E

Eggs *(vegetarians only)*	38

F

Farfalle pasta	56
Fennel and citrus salad	71
Feta cheese	26, 51
Fruit compote	31
Fruit information	84
Fruit salads	83
Fusilli pasta	56

G

Goats cheese	35
Gooseberry crumble	78
Ginger and apricot trifle	88
Ginger, how to peel	79
Granola	33
Green vegetable cooking chart	64

H

Heating hobs chart	13
Herbs	8
Honey	iv
Hygiene	12

I

Introduction	iv

J

Jellies	81

K

Kale preparation	64
Kaffir lime leaf	60

L

Leek and potato soup	20
Lemon risotto	57
Lentils	46
Lentil chilli	45
Lentil salad	74
Left overs	12

M

Maple syrup	iv
Muesli	33
Mung bean casserole	65
Mushrooms (breakfast)	37
Mushroom soup	21
Mushrooms on toast	27

N

Naan breads	59
Nectarines	79
NHS guidelines	iv
Non-cook meals	25
Noodle and vegetable stir-fry	53
Nutrition	66

O

Onions, how to prepare	46
Onion gravy	62
Oven gloves	50
Oven temperatures	14

P

Pak choi	54
Pasta cooking tips	56
Pear	83
Pearl barley	66
Peppers (general)	42
Peppers, stuffed	41
Pilaf	51
Pine nuts	41
Pistachio nuts	87
Plum crumble	78
Plums (breakfast fruit)	34
Pomegranate seeds	87
Porridge	31, 32
Potatoes, baked	47, 48
Potatoes (in soup)	20
Puff pastry	44

Q

Quinoa	52, 74

R

Rhubarb crumble	77, 78
Rice	58, 73
Risotto	57
Roasting garlic	19
Roast vegetables	63

S

Sandwiches	28
Satsumas	71
Seasoning ingredients	7
Sausages, breakfast	37
Sausage barbecue skewers	61
Sausages and roast vegetables	63
Shallots, preparation	73
Shallots and beans	35
Snacks	24
Stages of progress	6
Steaming green vegetables	64
Stir frying	53, 54
Sugar snap peas	54
Super quick suppers	48
Sweet potato pie topping	49
Sweet chilli sauce	61

T

Thai vegetable curry	60
Timers	4
Tomato and avocado bruschetta	26
Tomato soup	19
Tomato tart	43
Tomato passata	49

T continued

Tomato pasta	53
Tomatoes on toast	27
Toast	27
Tortilla wraps	28
Trifle	87, 88
Tropical fruit salad	83

U

Understanding your cooker	13

V

Vegetable cooking tips	64
Vegetable curry	60
Vegetables roasted	
Vegetable stir fry	53, 54
Vegetable soup	17
Vegetable tart	44

W

Washing up	11, 12
Watercress	71
Water melon salads	86
Water melon treats	85
Weights and measures	14

Y

Young dandelion leaves	9, 70

Z

Zest of lemon	57
Zest of lime	85

Acknowledgements

- I am grateful to my son, Balavan, who showed me the need for this book.

- Thank you to my son Matthew for suggesting I could use the same format of recipe presentation that I had used previously in the 1960s for DATE magazine.

- Thank you to Rachael Todd for her help with information about vegan products.

- Thank you to Jo Rolfe for her thorough proof-reading.

- Thanks to friends and advisors who checked the book for omissions or mistakes.

- Thanks to Sharon Alward of Sharward Services Limited for her enthusiasm for this project and for her patience and skill while producing it.

- Thank you to the Tuesday Group at Hugh Websters Felixstowe Ferry Boatshed Studio for their interest and encouragement.

- Thank you for the constant support of friends and family.

Author Page

Born in 1933 Gill trained initially at Birmingham College of Art in the early fifties and then worked as an illustrator in Birmingham and London.

Working at Odhams Press in London in 1960 Gill illustrated a weekly cookery article for DATE magazine. The simple strip format she used then has been reused again in this book.

Gill married the artist Ray Thomas in 1955 and has two sons.

After a lifetime spent in education she became an advisory teacher for Hampshire County Council and later taught for a time at Reading University.

During her retirement in Suffolk Gill studied for her Fine Art Degree and gained her BA Hons at Suffolk University in 2008.

She continues to work as an illustrator and painter.

Throughout her lifetime Gill has enjoyed cooking for her family and friends, having absorbed her mother's enthusiasm for this useful and enjoyable life skill at an early age.